Princess Sophia's Gifts

Written by **Diane Hovey**

Illustrated by **Sara M. Butcher**

aHeARTT

alternative Healing Arts Resources, Therapy & Training
Diane Hovey
www.aheartt.com

Printed in China

First Edition

Princess Sophia's Gifts

This book is dedicated to my family, especially to Sonia who has brought wisdom to our family, and to all the wonderful people along our journey who have blessed our lives.

~ Diane Hovey

The illustrations in this book are a reflection of my faith in God and in honor of those who cultivate its growth, my family and dearest companion Brian. Without them the light in my work would not shine.

~ Sara M Butcher

The night Princess Sophia
was born the sky danced.

The people of the kingdom believed this third child of King Caradoc and Queen Raena, was a sign of good fortune. They brought gifts of jewelry, toys, blankets and songs for the Princess. Even Athena, the sage who lived in the hills and was rarely seen at the castle, brought Sophia a sapphire amulet.

Princess Sophia loved to climb trees, stairs, tables and chairs. She could be found running around the castle, weaving around her sister and brother, with the tail of a bogus mouse dangling from her mouth. She rode melons like a jousting champion and drew pictures like an artisan.

On her third birthday the townsfolk gave her a puppy. Princess Sophia and puppy Monet had fun tumbling down hills and playing dress-up. One day, they had a tea party with biscuits for Monet and teacakes for Sophia. A seed blew onto her teacake, but the princess did not notice it. The seed went down the wrong way. It hurt and made her cough and cough. Finally, her coughing stopped and the hurt went away. Sophia and Monet cuddled in the warm sun and watched ladybugs play hopscotch.

That night, while Sophia slept, the little seed began to move with each breath. Back and forth the seed moved from her lung to her throat, until it could no longer move. It was stuck.

Sophia coughed. The seed hurt. She trembled and tried to cry out, but could not make any sound. Sophia heard her mama coming to see what was wrong. Then everything faded away.

When Sophia opened her eyes she stood at the entrance to an exquisite garden. She looked in all directions for her mama and her papa, but they were nowhere to be seen.

Sophia stepped forward to enter the gate. A slender woman with long, flowing hair appeared. A warm glow surrounded her as she smiled at Sophia and extended her arms.

"Welcome Sophia, we have been waiting for you."

The woman took Sophia's hand and walked with her through the garden until they came to a little waterfall flowing into a crystal pool.

Sophia scrambled up the rock ledges by the pool and found the perfect spot. She bounced onto a velvety-blue pillow and the woman sat beside her.

"Sophia, we would like you to stay with us, but you must return to your home and family. However before you return, we have some special gifts for you because you will be a very important teacher."

Three more women appeared and rested on pillows near the princess. The first woman smiled at Sophia. She brought her hands together, raised them high, made a circle in the air, brought them back together and extended them toward Sophia. "Sophia, to you I offer the gift of beauty."

This was a strange gift. No package, bows, toys or even clothes. Yet somehow Sophia knew this was very special. She smiled.

The third woman turned toward Sophia and firmly, but gently, held her hands without speaking until Sophia was certain an entire day had passed. Even though it seemed forever, Sophia did not wiggle or even squirm, for the touch of the woman's hands was calming and comforting.

"Sophia, to you I give the gift of patience and endurance."

The three women who gave Sophia gifts disappeared as quickly as they had appeared. Only the woman who first greeted her remained.

"Are you ready to go home now?"

Sophia nodded and asked, "Can I come back?"

"Not for a while, but we will meet here again someday." The woman knelt in front of Sophia, gathered her in her arms, and kissed her on her forehead.

Weeks later Sophia awoke to her mama's voice softly singing, She recognized her mama's voice but her past was only a hazy memory. Everything was new to her.

Their little princess who once charmed everyone in the kingdom could no longer walk, talk or make people gasp at the sight of a mouse in her mouth. The seed she swallowed had stopped her breath and caused great damage.

The King, Queen, Princess Lynette and Prince Edward cried to have Sophia back the way she was. They were sure she would walk and talk again, if only they tried hard enough, if only they prayed long enough, if only they found the right cure. They could not rest until the answers were found.

So, the whole royal family packed their bags and set out with Princess Sophia on a quest.

Across vast prairies, over towering mountains, and through dark tunnels they traveled, seeking wise people to give them answers and find a cure for Sophia. The seasons passed. When cold winds began to blow the family knew it was time to return home with Sophia where the warmth of her laughter could once again fill the castle.

Athena, the sage, greeted the royal family on their return to the castle. "Come," she said, "I have warm bread and soup."

Nothing had ever tasted so good. After dinner, Athena said "Tell me what you found on your journey."

"We found many wonderful people," said Queen Raena, "and Sophia enchanted them all."

"Did you find the answers you were searching for?"

They shook their heads, sadly no. Yet the King smiled and replied, "We learned not all questions have answers."

"Indeed. And who have you brought home with you?"

Prince Edward tussled his little sister's hair as he answered, "No one, just us." Sophia laughed with her spirited charm.

"Have you not?" Athena challenged.

Princess Lynette looked at Sophia as her little sister squeezed her hand. She declared, "Oh Sophia we went in search of a cure as though we had lost you, but we didn't."

Athena sighed, "Yes indeed, you have returned richly blessed with wisdom."

Sophia smiled. She knew all along she had never been lost.

Years passed. Princess Sophia's beauty grew
beyond measure. Some believed that a princess
who could not walk or talk was a bad omen. But,
those who came to know the princess felt their
hearts blossom with understanding. They knew
Sophia's joy and invincible spirit shed light so
others' gifts could shine.

Author's Notes

We all have stories to tell. It is part of being human.

Stories can help us understand life events from a new perspective. It allows us to honor our life experiences while revealing the wisdom we have gained in these experiences.

At its essence, *Princess Sophia's Gifts* is a true story. It grew out of my need to tell my daughter's story in a way that could build understanding. My daughter did indeed choke, when she was only 14 months old. A kernel lodged in her lung and we had no idea it was there. Gravity kept it at the bottom of her lung, but at night when she was lying down, it moved with her breathing causing swelling and then blockage. She woke with a strange sounding cough and then stopped breathing. When paramedics arrived, she had no vital signs. Twenty-five minutes passed before she was brought back to life. This unbelievable amount of time without oxygen caused significant brain damage. As a result, our daughter is very physically limited. She is however, beautiful and delightful. She has a great sense of humor and doesn't want to miss a minute of life. Her name Sonia is a form of Sophia, meaning wisdom. I gave her this name because I wanted her to be a strong, wise woman. Little did we know the ways she would bring so much wisdom into life.

Business Info:
Diane Hovey, PhD, CPT
alternative Healing Arts Resources, Therapy & Training
www.aheartt.com